RENOIR
COLOUR & NATURE

BY

DAVID SPENCE

THE WORLD OF RENOIR

*P*ierre Auguste Renoir was born in Limoges, France, on 25 February 1841. His father, Leonard Renoir, was a tailor; his mother, Marguerite Merlet, a dressmaker. The family moved to the Louvre area of Paris when Pierre was just four years old, making home at 23 Rue d'Argenteuil. Leonard, Marguerite and their five children shared the Paris apartment which Re[noir] later recalled as the size of a 'pocket handkerchief'. Leonard continued business as a tailor from the Rue d'Argenteuil apartment, his tailor's bench being transformed into his own bed at night. Renoir was the second youngest so gradually, as his elder brothers Henri and Victor found jobs and moved out of the family home, the pressure on space eased. The family lived in the very centre of Paris and could observe from their windows the riots of 1848 which led to the Revolution, which in turn installed Louis Napoleon Bonaparte as President of the Republic of France and then Emperor. Renoir grew up in a city being transformed by revolutions of state, industry and, most, importantly of all, culture.

Detail showing Renoir's portrait.

PORTRAIT OF 43 PAINTERS IN THE STUDIO OF GLEYRE, c.1862

In 1862, at the age of twenty-one, Renoir was accepted at the École des Beaux-Arts to study art. He was an average pupil frustrated as many of the students were by the unadventurous traditional teac[hing] methods with their dependence on studies from models of antiquity. From 1861 Renoir had attended c[lasses at] the private studio of the Swiss painter, Charles Gleyre. Many young hopefuls were attracted to Gleyre's s[tudio and] teaching which was far more liberal than the established schools despite the fact that Gleyre's own painti[ng did] not manage to raise itself above the average. Renoir's fellow pupils included Claude Monet, Alfred Sisle[y and] the talented Frédéric Bazille who was tragically to die in the Franco-Prussian war. This group portrait of 43 painters in Gleyre's studio includes a portrait of Renoir, painted by his friend Emile-Henri Lapo[rte].

BATHERS IN THE SEINE (LA GRENOUILLÈRE), 1869

This painting by Renoir is one of four he made of the subject. He painted the scene *en plein-air* (outdoors) on site. Claude Monet was another painter of the time who went to La Grenouillère to paint. Monet described his plans in a letter to Bazille; *'I have a dream, a picture, the bathers at La Grenouillère. I have done some poor sketches for it, but it is only a dream. Renoir, who has just spent two months here, also wants to paint this motif.'*

ISLAND BAL DE LA GRENOUILLÈRE

The bathing pools at La Grenouillère, just 20 minutes by train from the central Paris station of Saint-Lazare, were a popular day trip destination for Parisians relaxing on weekends or holidays. Although La Grenouillère translates as 'frog-pond' the name had nothing to do with any frogs that may have lived in the ponds. 'Frogs' was the name given by men to the girls who spent the summers at the pools and who had a reputation for being flirtatious. Renoir described the 'frogs' as being *'very good sorts'* and found several models who would pose for him among the bathers at La Grenouillère.

THE PORCELAIN PAINTER

At the age of thirteen Renoir was apprenticed to a porcelain painter decorated vases and plates. His brother, Henri, was already established engraver and Renoir's family encouraged their children in their c trades, eager no doubt to see some money coming in to the ily home. Renoir experimented with decorative painting on fans and furniture as well as porcelain. This vase, painted by Renoir when he was an apprentice, is decorated with figures based on Jean Goujon's *Nymphs*.

INFLUENCES & EARLY WORKS:
ROMANCE & REALISM

PORTRAIT OF
ROMAINE LACAUX
(detail), 1864

This portrait of the daughter of a porcelain manufacturer is one of Renoir's earliest commissioned paintings, as well as one of his most accomplished. Painted when he was only twenty-four years old, Renoir has managed to capture the freshness of youth and clear-eyed innocence of the young Romaine.

Renoir's grounding in painting began as a commercial artist painting figures and scenes on porcelain until this craft was made redundant by the introduction of machine printing. This early experience of copying classical figures and rococo scenes helped Renoir acquire skills which he retained all his working life, as well as developing a lasting interest in the work of the classical masters. His early career as a painter, however, began with his studentship under Charles Gleyre, and continued with his admiration of the works of 19th-century French artists Eugène Delacroix and Gustave Courbet. In 1848 Courbet had caused a stir in the ar world with his realistic paintings depicting simple everyday scenes, such as road-mending peasants breaki stones. This realism reflected Courbet's view of the world and art's place within it, and was a break from traditional subjects thought suitable for art, such as scenes from antiquit painted in a formal classical style. Courbet's break with tradition made possible for artists such as Édouard Manet concentrate on realistic scenes and began t free artists from the tyranny of tradition.

WOMEN OF ALGIERS

Eugène Delacroix

Delacroix was considered a great artist even in his own time. His painting was very influential during the first half of the 19th century. He was a champion of Romantic art which represented uncontrolled nature, including 'human nature' or actions, as opposed to the tradition of classicism which represented fixed ideas of behaviour and standards of beauty. Romanticism was therefore considered 'modern' and attracted modern-thinking artists. Romantic art sometimes looked towards Oriental subject matter which was considered exotic and exciting.

THE STONE-BREAKERS

Gustave Courbet

Courbet believed that artists should only paint '*real and existing things*'. It led to the conclusion that artists should only believe what they could see with their own eyes. This meant painting the people and scenes they could see around them exactly as they appeared, not how they were taught to imagine they should be. Ordinary people in modern dress became the subject matter, and light and its impression on the scene became important. What better way to get closer to the 'truth' than to take the easel and painting to the subject rather than bring the subject to the studio?

WOMAN OF ALGIERS *(detail)*

In 1870 Renoir painted this portrait of a woman of Algiers, heavily influenced by the oriental style that was fashionable at the time. It owes much to Delacroix's painting of the same subject but Renoir's painting has made the transition an imaginary scene to a very real one. Delacroix's paintings were inated by Romantic notions of exoticism relying on imaginary ay places. Renoir's *Woman of Algiers*, dressed in an exotic and ful costume, is depicted as a very real woman. The model ually Renoir's nineteen-year-old girlfriend Lise Trehot ectly engages the viewer's gaze in a very sensual way. By placing her in an Oriental costume rather than ntemporary French dress Renoir does not offend his viewer's idea of how women should behave.

INFLUENCES & EARLY WORKS:
IMPRESSIONISM

*R*enoir's fellow pupils at Charles Gleyre's studio, Monet, Bazille and Sisley, all continued to work together after Gleyre's retirement in 1864. Monet persuaded them to travel to Fontainebleau to paint directly from nature. Renoir's first submission to the official Paris Salon annual exhibition of painting in 1864 was entitled *Esmeralda Dancing* a Goat. The fact that the picture was accepted tells us a lot about the paint because the work of the Realists and Impressionists were continually reject by the Salon. No record exists of this painting because Renoir later destroy it on the grounds that it contained asphalt and would not last, although pos it was because he was not content with the way it appeared. Renoir and fellow painters had set about painting the world around them – the Paris st scenes, local bathing spots, boating on the river Seine and scenes from the and music halls. In 1874 the Société Anonyme des Artistes formed to ex their pictures, independent from the official Salon, The fir exhibition contained works by Monet, Morisot, Renoir Degas, Cézanne, Pissarro and Sisley. The group became known as the Impressionists.

THE POPPY FIELD AT ARGENTEUIL

Claude Monet

This picture was painted by Monet in 1873, the year before the first Impressionist exhibition. It shows two pairs of figures walking through a poppy field near his home at Argenteuil on a warm summer's day and has become one of Impressionism's best-known images. Renoir visited Monet at Argenteuil and they went out into the surrounding countryside to paint. Monet and Renoir shared lodgings together when they were young and poor. Renoir later explained that they spent all their money on studio rent, models and coal for the stove to keep the model warm. They would time their cooking with their painting so the hot stove both warmed the model and cooked the food.

COUNTRY FOOTPATH IN THE SUMMER, 1874

This picture of figures walking along a country footpath painted in 1874 is full of the sunlight which filled Monet's landscapes. The scene is remarkably similar to Monet's painting of the Argenteuil poppy fields and shows Renoir as a true adherent to Impressionist painting at that time. When the Impressionists mounted their second exhibition in 1876 at Durand-Ruel's gallery in the Rue le Peletier, Renoir was represented by 15 pictures. Although Impressionism still had its critics Renoir managed to sell six pictures and was finding admirers such as the publisher Georges Charpentier who commissioned Renoir to paint a family portrait. This relative success enabled Renoir to rent a house and gave him a degree of stability which allowed him to concentrate on his art.

LISE *(detail)*, 1868

Renoir had some early successes with paintings being accepted by the official Salon in the 1860s, such as this portrait of Lise. This painting of girlfriend Lise Trehot was unusual in that it was full length, a convention normally reserved for royalty. Artist and critic Zacharie Astruc described Lise as '*the daughter of the people, with all her typical Parisian features*'.

One reaction to the picture was; '*The whole thing is so natural and has been observed so accurately that it will appear wrong…we are used to imagining nature in terms of conventional colours.*' The painting was purchased by the writer Theodore Duret for 1,200 francs.

THE ARTIST'S LIFE
THE ART OF HIS DAY

Renoir's career as a painter developed alongside the Impressionists who are so well known today. Their depictions of comfortable middle class scenes either in the Parisian streets or surrounding countryside differed from the earlier Realist imagery such as Millet's peasant scenes, but nevertheless sought to paint pictures of real life as they experienced it. Many of Renoir's contemporaries, however, continued to paint in the traditional way, depicting religious or mythological scenes in a highly finished style. These artists found continued acceptance at the official Salon where their paintings were exhibited. The Impressionist's paintings with their sketchy unfinished style and modern subject matter were considered too shocking to be exhibited at the Salon where the unsuspecting French public might see them. The technology of the day also had an impact on the development of Impressionism. The growing number of newspapers and journals circulated wider and wider thanks

to more efficient and cheaper reproduction methods, and an increasingly literate public were able to read about the latest art, and see reproductions. The movement even owed its name to a journalism. A review by critic Louis Léroy referred to the 'Exhibition of Impressionists' in the magazine *Le Charivari*.

THE GULF OF MARSEILLES

Paul Cézanne

Paul Cézanne was the son of a hat-maker who moved into banking and became a we_ citizen of his home town of Aix-en-Proven_ Cézanne studied art in Paris where he met Pissarro and the circle of Impressionist painters with whom he exhibited in 1874. He met and fell in love with artist's model Hortense Fiquet in Paris and they ha_ an illegitimate son whose existence Cézanne kept from his parents. When they discovered the truth the_ halved his allowance leaving the family to borrow money where they could. When Cézanne inherited _ father's fortune he concentrated on painting in Provence, concerning himself with form and space, ma_ 'something solid' of Impressionism.

LE PONT DE L'EUROPE

Gustave Caillebotte

Gustave Caillebotte was a wealthy collector of Impressionist paintings and a talented artist in his own right. His work was not considered to be as important as the Impressionists but in the 1960s his art was 'rediscovered' and is now very popular. Caillebotte painted domestic everyday scenes of Paris life using dramatic perspective and a more highly finished technique than his Impressionist friends. There is an overwhelming sense of modernism in his paintings, stressed by the open air 'snapshot' feeling as if the image has been captured through the lens of ...era. His paintings were respected by his friends and contemporaries ...ere exhibited at the Impressionist exhibition of 1876. Caillebotte ...p a large collection of Impressionist paintings including ten by ...ir, often buying them from friends at inflated prices in order to ...rt them. In his will he left his collection to the State on the ...tion that they be exhibited at the Louvre. When he died in 1894 ...ore conservative artists protested that if the State accepted his ...tion it would be a sign of moral decline and the end of the nation. ...ually 38 of the 57 paintings were exhibited, supposedly on the ...ds of a lack of space at the Louvre.

THE LIFE OF RENOIR

~1841~
Born on 25 February
at Limoges, France

~1844~
Renoir family move to Paris

~1854~
Renoir becomes an
apprentice at Levy Brothers,
painting plates and vases

~1858~
Made redundant by new
technique for printing
onto porcelain

~1862~
Studies at Charles
Gleyre's studio
where he meets
Sisley, Monet
and Bazille

PORTRAIT OF JULIE MANET

Berthe Morisot

Berthe Morisot's truly Impressionist paintings of elegant Parisian women are notable for their freshness and delicacy. Morisot was able to paint the crisp starched linen and soft silk of evening dress with blurred brushstrokes which are dragged across the surface of the canvas retaining their immediacy of touch. The 'impression' of having captured the fleeting ...oment as a woman prepares to dress for the ...ening or, interrupted, glimpses towards the ...iewer, makes her a true Impressionist. ...risot married Édouard Manet's brother, ...ugene, and they had a daughter, Julie, who appears in a number of the Impressionist group's paintings including those by Renoir.

THE LIFE OF RENOIR

~1864~
Has a painting
accepted by the Salon
but later destroys it

~1865~
Meets Lise Trehot who
becomes his girlfriend
and model

~1872~
Has two paintings purchased
by dealer Durand-Ruel
and spends the summer
painting with Monet

~1874~
Exhibits at the first
Impressionist show

~1880~
Meets Aline Charigot

~1881~
Travels to
Algeria, Venice,
Rome and Naples

~1883~
Experiments with
new 'Dry Style'
of painting

~1885~
Birth of his son Pierre

~1888~
First attack of rheumatoid
arthritis which leaves his
face partially paralysed

~1892~
Young Girls at the Piano
purchased by the State

~1894~
Birth of son Jean

~1890~
Marries Aline Charigot

~1901~
Birth of son Claude (Coco)

Renoir's second son, Jean, was born on 15 September 1894. In Jean Renoir's own memoirs of his father he writes that his mother exclaimed on his birth; '*Heavens how ugly, take it away!*' Jean became a famous film director as well as a writer of several books, including a biography of his father. Another witness to Jean's birth was Gabrielle Renard, the fifteen-year-old cousin of Aline Charigot who had come from her home in Essoyes to help with the preparations for the birth. Gabrielle stayed to help look after Jean. She became Renoir's favourite model, at first posing with the children such as in this portrait with Jean, but in Renoir's later years she became an important figure in Renoir's exploration of the female form in such paintings as *Gabrielle with Jewel Box* (page 24). Ga continued as Renoir's pr model until 1914 wh married and left the home in C

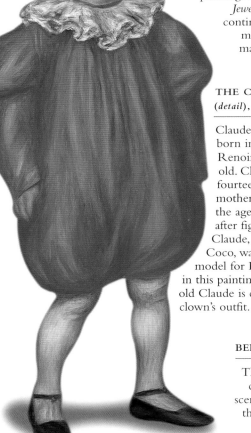

THE CLOWN
(detail), 1909

Claude Renoir was born in 1901 when Renoir was sixty years old. Claude was only fourteen when his mother, Aline, died at the age of fifty-six, after fighting diabetes. Claude, nicknamed Coco, was often a model for Renoir and in this painting the six-year-old Claude is dressed in a clown's outfit.

DÉJEUNER A BERNEVAL, C.1905

This is a charming domestic interior scene, at home with the Renoir family.

FAMILY, FRIENDS & OTHERS

Renoir did not come from a comfortable middle class family as did many of his Impressionist friends. His father's tailoring business was just sufficient to support the family and Renoir found a job as an apprentice to a porcelain painter when he was thirteen to supplement the family income. When he decided to study painting at the studio of Charles Gleyre he soon became friends with Claude Monet, éric Bazille and Alfred Sisley. He kept company this artistic circle and had many girlfriends ng the models who posed for his paintings, but us not until Renoir was nearly forty that he met e Charigot, a nineteen-year-old dressmaker who nearby Renoir's home in the Rue Saint-Georges.

BUST OF MADAME RENOIR WITH PIERRE

Aline posed for Renoir and fell in love with him despite her mother's advice to find a man who was old and wealthy. Aline travelled to Italy with Renoir in 1881 and much later referred to the trip as their 'honeymoon', despite the fact they were not actually married until 1890.

Aline Charigot came from the Burgundy area of France and was teased by her Parisian friends about her accent and country ways. When they first met, Renoir and Aline spent much of their time together by the river Seine, travelling by train from Saint-Lazare to the Chatou bridge and then the Fournaise restaurant. Renoir's well known painting *Luncheon of the Boating Party* (page 17) depicts a scene at the Fournaise restaurant which shows Aline holding a small dog. Aline moved in with Renoir after his return from a trip to Algeria in 1881. Their first child, Pierre, was born in 1885. Renoir found a studio near the family apartments in the Rue Houdon in order that, according to Aline, '*the baby will be able to cry to his heart's content.*' Pierre became an actor but went to fight in the First World War were he was badly wounded.

FAMILY, FRIENDS & OTHERS

The small group of friends who studied together under Charles Gleyre and then continued to paint together were at the very centre of the movement which was subsequently named Impressionism. In 1865 Renoir shared a studio with Alfred Sisley and a year later, after Sisley was married, he moved in with Frédéric Bazille, a talented young painter who was tragically killed at the age of twenty-nine during the Franco-Prussian war.

In 1867 Bazille rented a Paris studio at 20 rue Visconti. From here he wrote to his mother; *'Since my last letter there is something new at the rue Visconti. Monet has fallen from the sky with a collection of huge canvases which will be a grea success at the World Fair. He will stay here unti the end of the month. With Renoir that makes needy painters that I'm housing. It's a veritabl sanatorium. I'm delighted, I have plenty of sp and both are very good company.'* Renoir a Bazille continued to be close friends, l moving together to a studio near the famous Café Guerbois which becam the meeting place for the new wave modern-thinking artists such as Ma Monet, Degas, and Pissarro, as we writers like Émile Zola, Edmond Duranty and Zacharie Astruc.

PORTRAIT OF JULIE MANET (detail), c.1

Julie Manet often stayed with the Renoir fai particularly after the death of her parents, Berthe Morisot and Eugène Manet, which left her orphaned at the age of seventeen. Morisot had asked Renoir to look after Julie although her official guardian was the poet Stéphane Mallarmé.

MADAME ALPHONSE DAUDET *(detail)*, 1875

Alphonse Daudet was a successful novelist and playwright who was regarded as one of the leading members of the Realist movement in literature together with writers such as Émile Zola. Daudet was a great supporter of Impressionism, commissioning this portrait of his wife and buying works from a number of other artists. Daudet was a frequent visitor to the Nouvelle-Athènes café, mixing with the artistic set who met to talk about their work. He was also often invited to Renoir's house where he would join the likes of Zola, Odilon Redon and Stéphane Mallarmé for dinner.

PORTRAIT OF CLAUDE MONET *(detail)*, 1875

Claude Monet moved to Argenteuil, a suburb of Paris, in 1871. Renoir was amongst the many visitors that stayed with Monet at Argenteuil. When they were together Monet persuaded Renoir to take up his easel and go out into the countryside to paint, *en plein-air*. Several of Renoir's paintings are of views of the Seine such as the picture of racing boats entitled *The Seine at Argenteuil*. Renoir also made numerous portraits of his friend Claude Monet and Claude's wife Camille. Monet's obsession with capturing in paint the changing moods of his subject matter according to the light made him the leading exponent of Impressionism. In his own words, Monet wanted to *'ensnare the light, and throw it directly on to the canvas'*.

PORTRAIT OF RICHARD WAGNER, 1882

Renoir was introduced to Wagner's music by a friend at a time when national sentiment was against the composer. This made Renoir determined to like his music and Renoir was eventually introduced to Wagner in person, at which time he made three sketches, (executed in under an

and this portrait. During the meeting Wagner
ed to offend the artist because of his
of French composers whom Wagner
Renoir expressed his like for the music
enbach which Wagner dismissed as
usic, but not bad'. Later on Renoir
ed a performance of Wagner's
Die Walküre at Bayreuth, and
ented; *'They have no right to
ople up in the dark for three solid
.you are forced to look at the only
here there is any light; the stage.
olute tyranny…We might as well be
bout it; Wagner's music is boring.'*

LE MOULIN DE LA GALETTE, 1876

The painting, which has been described as the most beautiful picture of the 19th century, appears at first glance to be chaotic. The foreground and background merge and the overlapping forms of the figures are often indistinguishable. The sunlight that filters through the foliage casts shadows that fall across the figures and ground alike, creating a dappled effect that unifies the picture.

Renoir made many studies from models for his figures in *Le Moulin de la Galette*. The two young girls in the centre of the picture, one resting her arm on the other's shoulder, are Jeanne and Estelle, seamstresses known as 'grisettes,' dressed in the latest Paris style. Renoir described how he saw Jeanne on the streets of Montmartre, thought her the ideal model, and stopped and spoke to her. *'I don't go in for that sort of thing Monsieur,'* she replied. Renoir noted that; *'She had lovely hands, the ends of her fingers were swollen from being pricked by needles.'* Eventually Renoir persuaded Jeanne's mother to let her daughter pose for him in return for payment, and soon Jeanne's sister Estelle also became Renoir's model.

The pair of dancers depicted centre-left is the Cuban painter Pedro Vidal with Margot Legrand. Margot appears to be the same young girl who Jean Renoir recalls was nursed by his father and Dr Gachet, but she died of suspected small-pox three years after this picture was painted.

WHAT DO THE PAINTINGS SAY?

PARIS SOCIETY

The pipe smoker (on the right) is Norbert Goeneutte and seated next to him with pen poised is writer Georges Rivière.

*T*he years before the end of the 19th century are known in France as the Belle Époque, the golden age when life was for the enjoying. This description does not convey the fact that it was also the time when many were struggling for equal rights such as workers and women in general. Nevertheless it was a time when Paris prospered with new roads, railways and buildings and the middle classes became more secure and prosperous. Mass entertainment was available in the form of the café-concerts and dance halls, the most popular of which was the *Folies-Bergère* which still exists today. Renoir painted modern Parisian life. Images of young people at play, in the park, the dance hall, strolling along the boulevards show us the pleasant side of Paris life. Renoir was e that he concentrated on the nice things when he said *'There are enough asant things in this world. We don't have to paint them as well.'* Although Renoir entrated on the pleasant side of life he painted es from the ordinary everyday world of the ian worker at play, not the fashionable -to-do classes, and it is this record of real life that makes his painting fascinating.

DANCING AT THE MOULIN DE LA GALETTE

A building programme in the 1860s and 1870s transformed the landscape of Paris. Some of the surrounding parishes became part of the city as it grew and grew. Montmartre had been a village on a hill with windmills and vineyards, before it was swallowed-up by Paris. The fashion for public dances in the 1870s meant that nearly every available space in Paris, from bars and courtyards to squares and parks, were at some time used for this new craze. The best-known dance-bar in Montmartre was le Moulin de la Galette, or 'le Radet' for short. It had an outdoor dance floor as well as a bar for red wine and 'galettes', a kind of circular waffle from which it gained its name.

FAMOUS IMAGES

By the end of the 1870s Renoir was no longer exhibiting with the Impressionists and had decided to follow his own individual course. When he painted the *Luncheon of the Boating Party* in 1881 he had already made a break with Impressionism. He stated that *'I had wrung Impressionism dry, and I finally came to the conclusion that I neither knew how to paint nor draw. In a word, Impressionism was a blind alley.'* His tours of Algeria and then Italy gave him new inspiration and new direction, and he re-discovered the works of the Old Masters. The style employed in the execution of the *Luncheon of the Boating Party* is more assured than th of *Le Moulin de la Galette* painted five yea earlier. The individual figures portrayed more clearly defined, particularly by th use of stronger colour, and the forms appear to be gaining greater form and solidity.

YOUNG WOMAN WITH A FAN (*detail*), 1881

This portrait of Alphonsine, daughter of restaur owner Alphonse Fournaise, captures the charm which made her a favoured model with mar male admirers. She features in *Luncheon of the Boating Party*, leaning against the rail.

THE LUNCHEON OF THE BOATING PARTY, 1880/1

The scene depicted in this well-known painting is the Restaurant Fournaise on the Ile de Chatou, a little island in the river Seine near the Ile de Croissy. It was a short train ride from Renoir's studio in the centre of Paris. The owner of the restaurant, Alphonse Fournaise, had built a landing stage for the Parisians who wished to swim and hire boats on the river, and he began to serve refreshments on the stage. Renoir recalls the place *'where life was a perpetual holiday and the world knew how to laugh in those days.'* Renoir often used to visit the Restaurant Fournaise with his girlfriend Aline.

The figure wearing a top hat and engaged in conversation at the back of the scene is banker and art collector Charles Ephrussi.

In the background is Paul Lhote holding actress Jeanne Samary by the waist.

Aline Charigot, Renoir's future wife, sits at the table holding a small dog. Behind is Alphonse Fournaise, the restaurant owner.

The seated figure wearing the straw hat is painter Gustave Caillebotte who talks to actress Ellen Andrée.

RENOIR'S FRIENDS

The painting shows many of Renoir's friends, several of whom sat for Renoir in his studio so he could finish the picture. The group is notable for its social mix, with flower sellers and bankers drinking side by side. The relaxed scene is full of meaningful glances and intimate touches. The arrangement of figures around a table laden with fruit and wine suggests there is more to the picture than simply a group portrait of Renoir's acquaintances.

THE UMBRELLAS, 1881/5

This painting clearly demonstrates Renoir's different approaches to painting in the 1880s. The artist returned to this painting again and again over a period of years. The figures on the right of the picture are painted in Renoir's 'Impressionist' style of the 1870s with bright colours but soft outlines and looser brushstrokes. The two figures on the left however were painted in a later style which has more clearly defined outlines, a more 'finished' surface and more subdued colours.

It is thought that the painting was begun around 1881 because the right-hand figures are wearing dresses and hats that were fashionable at that time, and Renoir normally dressed his models in the latest fashions. By 1883 simpler dresses came into style and the woman holding a basket is dressed in a style which was the height of fashion in 1885, but which had fallen out of fashion by 1887. Recent X-ray examination of the painting suggests that the woman on the left was first painted in the earlier Impressionist method around 1881 with skirts similar to the other women in the picture, complete with white lace cuffs and collar and a hat. This figure was over-painted in about 1885.

DETECTION THROUGH COLOU

Further examination *The Umbrellas* reveals the pr of cobalt blue pigment ir right hand section of the pi and in the original painting underneath the left-hand figures. pigment was used by Renoir only during the 1870s and early French Ultramarine, a pigment used later by Renoir, was fo in the colours on the left-hand figures we see today. He a experimented with removing the oil medium and replacing with a water-based medium to bind the colours because he thought the oil would eventually darken and spoil his colours, although this experiment was without success. This examination of the use of pigments and medium enables art historians to find out the history of the painting.

HOW WERE THEY MADE?
THE DRY STYLE

When Renoir visited Italy in 1881 he went to see the art of the great masters such as Michelangelo, Raphael and Bernini. He later recalled that he became tired of the draped figures with too many folds and muscles, and preferred the Pompeiian frescoes in the Naples Museum. He marvelled at the wonderful colours achieved by the fresco painters with such a limited range of colours made from earths and vegetable dyes, and even confessed to repairing a wall painting using paints in powder form that he found in a nearby mason's house. The experience of Renoir's Italian trip was certainly one factor that made him change the way he was painting. By 1883 Renoir openly admitted that Impressionism was a dead end and that he was looking for a new style. He rejected the Impressionist way of painting outdoors, stating that *'An artist who paints straight from nature is really only looking for nothing but momentary effects. He does not try to be creative himself, and as a result the pictures soon become monotonous.'* Renoir's exploration of new ways of painting in the 1880s have now become known as his 'Dry Period'.

THE SCHOOL OF ATHENS *(detail)*

Raphael

Renoir's gradual disillusionment with the Impressionist style of rapidly building-up the surface of the canvas with touches of colour was hastened by what he saw on his trip to Italy. He admired the purity and grandeur of Raphael's wall-paintings which retained bright colourful surfaces and were masterful compositions with great clarity of structure and form.

19

WHAT DO THE PAINTINGS SAY?

A NEW DIRECTION

Renoir's 'Dry Period' is also sometime known as his 'Ingresque' period aft the famous French painter Jean Ing Ingres was a dominant influence i French painting in the earlier part of the 19th century. Ingres spent a good part of his career Italy and was a devoted follower of the art of Raphael great Italian painter of the High Renaissance. The ar Ingres, in his admiration of Raphael, was in turn ad by Renoir. This direct line of influence exten back to Raphael's source of inspiration; th great classical art of ancient Greece. In pur this new direction in his painting Renoir w rejecting the modern art of Impressionism wh he felt had lost its way. He was returning to the traditional values which had remained unchanged for centuries. Renoir became interested in the methods of Renaissance artists and he criticized the modern teaching methods which had replaced the apprenticeship system. The culmination of his new direction was a large painting called *The Bathers*.

THE BLONDE BATHER

This painting was made by Renoir in 1887 at the heigh his 'Dry Period'. The influence of Ingres is quite evide formal pose of the figure against a classical landscape re the fresco paintings Renoir had visited during his trip t The painting resembles fresco painting because of its bri colouring, smooth finish and clear edges around the fema form. However Renoir does not resist breaking-up the land with individually applied brushstrokes. About this time a cr asked Renoir whether he considered himself a descend of Ingres, to which Renoir replied *'I only wish I was.'*

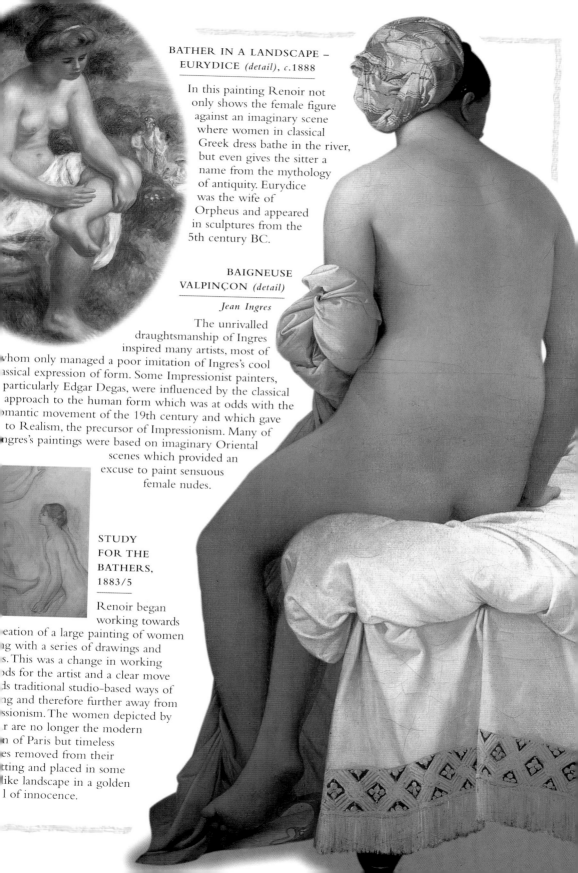

BATHER IN A LANDSCAPE – EURYDICE (detail), *c.*1888

In this painting Renoir not only shows the female figure against an imaginary scene where women in classical Greek dress bathe in the river, but even gives the sitter a name from the mythology of antiquity. Eurydice was the wife of Orpheus and appeared in sculptures from the 5th century BC.

BAIGNEUSE VALPINÇON (detail)

Jean Ingres

The unrivalled draughtsmanship of Ingres inspired many artists, most of whom only managed a poor imitation of Ingres's cool classical expression of form. Some Impressionist painters, particularly Edgar Degas, were influenced by the classical approach to the human form which was at odds with the Romantic movement of the 19th century and which gave [rise] to Realism, the precursor of Impressionism. Many of Ingres's paintings were based on imaginary Oriental scenes which provided an excuse to paint sensuous female nudes.

STUDY FOR THE BATHERS, 1883/5

Renoir began working towards [the cr]eation of a large painting of women [bathing] with a series of drawings and [studies]. This was a change in working [meth]ods for the artist and a clear move [toward]s traditional studio-based ways of [worki]ng and therefore further away from [Impre]ssionism. The women depicted by [Renoi]r are no longer the modern [wome]n of Paris but timeless [figur]es removed from their [set]ting and placed in some [dream]like landscape in a golden [wor]l of innocence.

THE BATHERS

**THE GREAT BATHERS –
THE NYMPHS** *(detail)*

Renoir continued the theme of Bathers
from the 1880s to the end of his life.
This picture was painted about 1918,
when Renoir was seventy-seven years old.
The figures in the pastoral landscape appear
almost to be part of the ground upon which
they lie. They have a massiveness and solidity
which makes them appear like sculptures
modelled out of clay, but are painted in
striking flesh tones which are echoed in the
grass and the trees which surround them.
Renoir was racked by arthritis towards the
end of his life and was only able to paint
by having his paintbrushes wedged into
his bandaged hands. It was in this way
that the *Great Bathers* was painted.

enoir exhibited his
new paintings at the
Georges Petit Galler
They were exhibited
alongside paintings by artists such as
Monet, Pissarro, Morisot and Whistler,
and caused something of a stir because
of Renoir's departure from Impressionism
The painter Camille Pissarro, a friend of
Renoir, wrote to his son; *'Durand has bee
to Petits; he has seen the Renoirs, and doesn't
like his new style – he doesn't like it at all.'*
Durand-Ruel was an influential dealer
who had championed Impressionist art
and he was evidently discouraged to
find that one of his artists had now
adopted a different style of painting.
Pissarro commented on Renoir's new
style; *'I can quite understand the effort he is
making. It is a very good thing not to want t*
on repeating oneself, but he has concentrated all his effort on line. The figures stand
against each other without any sort of relationship and the whole thing is meaningles
Renoir is no draughtsman and without the lovely colours he used to use he is incohe

NYMPHS BATHING *François Girardon*

This bas-relief of nymphs bathing by the 17th-century artist François Girardon decorates one of the
fountain pools in the park of Versailles. Renoir found it a source of inspiration for his *Bathers* picture
as well as other works.

THE BATHERS

his painting was made over a period of several years and finally exhibited at Georges Petit's gallery n 1887. Renoir has created a picture which is completely unlike his former Impressionist works. e subject matter is drawn from a classical source and has none of the spontaneity in execution that ypifies Impressionism. In fact the pigment was spread with a knife and smoothed over as much as ssible to create a highly finished surface. The idealized beauty of the female forms in their carefully arranged poses have nothing to do with Paris in the 1880s and are divorced from any real or atural context. The women recall the porcelain decorations that Renoir made in his youth and the only real similarity with his earlier painting is the richness of colour, particularly in the surrounding landscape, which typifies Renoir's art.

DIANA BATHING

François Boucher

The Rococo style of the 18th century artist François Boucher was much admired by Renoir. Boucher's paintings of beautiful young women in classical landscapes were an obvious inspiration, as much for the subject matter as the style of painting.

GABRIELLE WITH JEWEL BOX, 1911

This painting made in 1910 shows Renoir's late style. The model is Gabrielle Renard, the young cousin of Renoir's wife Aline. Renoir was quite open about his fascination for women's bodies and talked about them in a way some would find unacceptable today.

To the artist they were objects to be observed and depicted: the quality of the skin compared to a fruit which must respond well to the light; the arrangement of the facial features must be in harmony *'with almond shaped eyes which should be half-way between the top of the head and the tip of the chin.'* Some critics think that this is why his models appear to be without spirit – they are painted as if they were fruit or flowers. Renoir's depiction of the female form is without lust. The women appear trance-like, increasingly detached from their surroundings.

BATHER WITH LONG HAIR
(detail), 1910

Renoir concentrated on voluptuous nudes who posed in a sea of vibrant colour, and it is almost as if his struggle with arthritis which gave him difficulty holding his paintbrushes allowed him the artistic freedom to relax his style, painting in a freer way with looser, broader brushstrokes. The female figures are as one with the landscape, and no longer appear to be conscious compositions, carefully arranged, but merge effortlessly with the background creating natural and sensuous imagery.

THE ARTIST'S VISION
HOW WERE THEY MADE?
THE LATE STYLE

THE JUDGEMENT OF PARIS

Peter Paul Rubens

In the 1890s Impressionist painting was becoming established in some circles, particularly with some [inf]luential collectors, but as a style [of] painting it was being surpassed [by] new styles such as the Symbolism [of] Paul Gauguin. Renoir by this time [wa]s an old man who suffered severe [att]acks of rheumatoid arthritis which [cri]ppled him and forced him to spend [the] winter months in the relative [wa]rmth of the South of France. [Fin]ally in 1905 he moved with his [fam]ily to Cagnes, a small town near [An]tibes on the Mediterranean coast. He had a house [buil]t which he called 'Les Collettes' which was to become [his] studio until his death. Towards the end of his life [his] arthritis was so severe that he was permanently wheelchair-bound and his hands became deformed to such an extent that he was unable to hold any object. He continued to paint with brushes wedged into his bandaged hands, and his pictures became more colourful then ever before.

Renoir's depiction of the female form developed and became more massive, taking on proportions which remind us of the 17th-century Dutch artist Rubens, and dominate the picture frame. The figures are completely timeless and might be from classical mythology or from the present day, but are isolated from everything except their landscape. The backgrounds are reduced to a field of colour, still Impressionistic in execution, and the whole is soaked in the Mediterranean sunlight which make the colours come alive.

CATHERINE HESSLING IN THE FILM NANA (right)

Catherine Hessling (also shown with Renoir in his studio) was a model who worked at the Nice Academie de Peinture and who went to work for Renoir when he was looking for models for his large *Great Bathers* painting. Dédée, as she was then known, travelled by train every day from Nice to Renoir's studio in Cagnes to pose for the artist. After Renoir's death in 1919 his son, Jean, married Dédée and she became an actress appearing in the early films directed by Jean Renoir under her stage name Catherine Hessling.

THE AUDIENCE FOR THE PICTURES

R enoir had no means of financial support except from odd jobs or from the sale of his paintings. At the beginning of his career as an arti times were hard. The society formed by the Impressionist group in 1873, with Renoir a member, had to be dissolved in 1875 due to large debts and the artists were forced to sell their pictures. They were auctioned at the Hotel Drouot in Paris on 24 March 1875 with disastrous results. With a hostile crowd and few buyers, Renoir sold twenty canvases for 2,000 francs compared to the 200,000 francs a respected Salon artist could earn for one painting alone. Early on Renoir depended on friends to purchase painti receiving support from Édouard Manet, Victor Chocquet and others. Chocquet was a civil servant in the Ministry of Finance who could ill afford to buy paintings. Renoir is reported to have said of him; *'What a charming crackpot...he scrap up the means to buy paintings from his salary...and never gave a thought to whet or not the art would appreciate in val*

PORTRAIT OF
DELPHINE LEGRAND *(detail)*, 1878

Some of the most charming of all Re work are his portraits of children. In picture of Delphine Legrand, daugh friend and art dealer Alphonse Leg Renoir is able to create a sense of innocence and vulnerability whic captures the spirit of the sitter.

NSIEUR AND MADAME BERNHEIM, 1910

The Bernheim family were art dealers who actively supported the Impressionist painters.

The Bernheims organised an important ibition for Renoir in 1900 and continued to present his work up to and beyond Renoir's death. During this time Renoir made several portraits of the Bernheim family members including this picture of Berheim-Jeune and his wife. The family was very rich, with a magnificent chateau, a house in Paris, a dozen motorcars, and even a dirigible balloon. Most importantly to Renoir, however, was that they had '*beautiful wives whose skins took to the light.*'

MADAME CHARPENTIER *(detail)*

In 1876 Renoir painted this portrait of Marguerite Charpentier, wife of Georges Charpentier, the publisher of famous novelists such as Flaubert, Zola and Maupassant. The family were very wealthy and had a reputation for gathering together the most interesting people of the day; writers, painters, composers, as well as actresses and popular singers. The Charpentiers supported Renoir as they did other artists, commissioning portraits of the family and using their influence ensure his paintings were exhibited, thereby giving r a degree of financial security. Renoir noted of the s with Marguerite Charpentier; '*She reminds me of ethearts of my youth, the models of Fragonard. The two rs had lovely dimples. I was congratulated. I forgot the of the newspapers. I had models who were willing to ee and who were full of goodwill.*'

PINK AND BLUE, 1881

Alice and Elizabeth Cahen d'Anvers were daughters of a wealthy banker. Renoir was commissioned to paint several portraits of the two girls after Charles Ephrussi, owner of the *Gazette des Beaux-Arts* had introduced Renoir to the Cahen family. It appears that the Cahens were disappointed with the double portrait and decided to hang it in the servants quarters, out of view of their friends.

NUDE IN THE
SUNLIGHT, 1876

In 1876 Durand-Ruel
exhibited Renoir's paintings at
the Rue le Pelletier, including
Nude in the Sunlight. The art
critic Albert Wolff wrote in
*Le Figaro; 'Try and explain to
Monsieur Renoir that a woman's
torso is not a mass of rotting flesh,
with violet-toned green spots all
over it, indicating a corpse in the
final stages of decay... And this
collection of vulgarities has been
exhibited in public without
a thought for possible fatal
consequences. Only yesterday a
poor man was arrested in the
Rue le Pelletier, after leaving the
exhibition, because he began
biting everyone in sight.'*

WHAT THE CRITICS SA

enoir's art has justifiably taken its pla
among the great Impressionist work
and he is considered today to be o
of the small group who changed th
course of art in the latter half of the 19th centur
Like his contemporary painters he found accepta
slow during his working life, but
towards the end of his career gained
recognition, fame and the money
that came with it. Renoir never
had any pretensions about his art.
He wanted to paint what he found
attractive and amusing, and by his
own admission did not dwell on
any concern to express great
ideas or emotions. He hated
any notion of artists being
more than simple labourers
who day after day had a job
to do – paint. This may be
because of his relatively
humble beginnings, but
whatever the reason critics
and especially art historians
in the 20th century have regarded his art as
somehow slighter, less important than his
contemporaries. By contrast the non-specialist
public at large have always found his art
attractive, accessible and enjoyable.

PORTRAIT OF A
YOUNG GIRL *(detail)*, 1888

Renoir's habit of making the eyes of his portrait subjects
dark in contrast to the surrounding pale face attracted
the attention of Arthur Baignieres, who wrote of
Renoir's painting *Mother and Children* in 1874;
*'From afar we see a bluish haze, from which six
chocolate drops forcefully emerge. Whatever could it
be? We come closer; the sweets are the eyes of three
people and the haze a mother and her daughters.'*

YOUNG GIRLS
AT THE PIANO, 1892

n 1892 the poet Stéphane
Mallarmé and the art critic
le Roger-Marx persuaded
enri Roujon, the Director
e Beaux-Arts, to purchase
a Renoir painting for the
te collection. An informal
nission resulted in Renoir
ting five versions of *Young
Girls at the Piano*. The state
chased one of the pictures
May 1892 for the sum of
francs. The State had only
ed paintings by one other
the original Impressionist
up, Alfred Sisley. Mallarmé
his support for Renoir in
letter to Roujon: *'It is my
feeling, as well as the agreed
opinion of everyone else, that
you cannot be sufficiently
congratulated on having
chosen such a definitive,
refreshing, bold work of
maturity for a museum.'*

Two years earlier
Renoir's friends had
asked on his behalf to
be decorated by the
State for his work
as a painter,
but Renoir
refused the
honour.

NEWS OF THE DIFFERENT EXHIBITIONS

There is an exhibition of the INTRANSIGENTS
(Impressionists) in the Boulevard des
Capucines, or rather, you might say, of the
LUNATICS, of which I have already given you
a report. If you would like to be amused, and
have a little time to spare, don't miss it.

At the time of the first Impressionist exhibitions the
press were very hostile. This article is from the paper
La Patrie on 14th May 1874

A PERFECT DAY

The quintessential Renoir image is a summer's day, pretty girls, wholesome food and a relaxed country setting. This imagery and the values it represents for today's audience have been adopted by the advertising industry.

Do you understand your own beauty? At our powder bar, the knowing consultant recognises the beauty that is yours alone. Even as you watch, she heightens your best points...from the face powder she hand-blends for your colouring to the fulfillment of *all* your beauty needs. Made-to-order face powder, pressed in a compact, $2; or boxed loose, $1.50, $2.50. All plus tax. At favoured department and speciality stores.

Charles of the Ritz

DURAND-RUEL

The art dealer Paul Durand-Ruel was influential in establishing Renoir's reputation. Durand-Ruel had been a long standing friend of Renoir and organized several solo exhibitions of his work, including a major retrospective of his work in 1892, and at his galleries in New York and the Grafton Galleries in London in 1905.

A LASTING IMPRESSION

*R*enoir died in 1919 at the age of seventy-eight. On the morning of his death he asked for paintbox and brushes despite being terribly ill with pneumonia. [s]on, Jean Renoir, wrote in his memoirs; *'He [...]ed the anenomes which Nenette, our kind-hearted [...], had gone out and gathered for him. For several [...] he identified himself with these flowers and forgot [...]ain. Then he motioned for someone to take his [...] and said "I think I am beginning to understand [...]thing about it." He died in the night.'* Even before [...]eath he had taken his place among the roll-[...] of great artists. His portrait of Madame [...]rpentier was acquired by the Louvre and he [...] fêted as his chair was wheeled through the [...]ries. His output was considerable; greater [...]aps then any of his fellow Impressionist [...]ters, having painted about 6,000 pictures. [...]y his works can be found in the major art [...]ries around the world, particularly in America [...]use American collectors acquired his pictures [...] they were still unfashionable in Europe.

ALBERT BARNES

One of Renoir's greatest patrons was Albert Barnes, an American millionaire and art collector. Barnes created the Barnes Foundation in 1922, an educational foundation and museum containing many Impressionist paintings as well as those by artists such as Manet and Matisse. The Foundation owns 180 paintings by Renoir, as well as 69 by Cézanne and 60 by Matisse. Barnes believed that Renoir's art was richer than that of his Impressionist contemporaries because he built upon the Impressionist style to develop a more perceptive style of painting. The Barnes Foundation originally restricted access to its collection but now the works are made available for loan to exhibitions.

LES COLLETTES & RENOIR'S STUDIO

Since 1960 Renoir's house at Cagnes-sur-Mer, Les Collettes, has been preserved by the Renoir Estate and the local government as a museum. It is surrounded by its 100-year-old olive grove and is a place of pilgrimage for Renoir students. Several works by

the artist are still at Les Collettes. Another location which has been preserved in memory of the artist is the Fournaise Restaurant on Chatou island in the Seine, known locally as the Impressionist's island. It is possible today to have lunch on the same terrace made famous in Renoir's masterpiece *Luncheon of the Boating Party.*

GLOSSARY

Porcelain - A ceramic material which is renowned for its translucent qualities and mainly used for manufacturing vases, cups and plates. It is made from kaolin (a type of clay) and a paste that includes substances such as soapstone and bone ash. The finished product is of fine quality and lends itself to decoration. Renoir started his career painting images on porcelain.

Rococo - This word derives form the French word *rocaille* (rock work) and is applied to a decorative style which became prominent in the early 18th century. France and Southern Germany are best known for architecture, painting and decorative arts which were made in the rococo style and which is exemplified by small curves, rounded forms and sometimes excessive ornamentation.

Gustave Courbet (1819-77) - An extremely influential artist who was largely self-taught and whose art was based on the rejection of idealization and Romanticism in favour of realism which he believed was truly democratic and 'noble'. His depictions of peasants working in the fields and stone quarries were largely unpopular but his work was admired by the new generation of Impressionists who valued his rejection of the classical in favour of his depiction of the real world around him.

Louvre - The most famous national museum and art gallery in France. Originally a Parisian royal palace built around 1546, it has been a venue for displaying art since 1793 and today attracts more visitors than any other museum or gallery in France.

Bas-relief - Relief is sculpture which is not free-standing but is similar to a painting with raised surfaces. The depth of the projections from the background determines the name given to a relief, normally cast in bronze or built up in plaster, clay or a similar material. High-relief (*alto-relievo*) has very deep projections compared with bas-relief (*basso-relievo*).

Belle époque - A French term to describe the period of life in the late 19th century and early 20th century up to the First World War. The belle époque (translated as 'fine period') was notable for its comfortable lifestyle free from major conflicts.

ACKNOWLEDGEMENTS

We would like to thank: Graham Rich and Elizabeth Wiggans for their assistance.
Copyright © 2004 *ticktock* Entertainment Ltd.
First published in Great Britain by *ticktock* Publishing Ltd.,
Unit 2, Orchard Business Centre, North Farm Road, Tunbridge Wells, Kent TN2 3XF.

A CIP catalogue record for this book is available from the British Library. ISBN 1 86007 484 7
Picture research by Image Select.
Printed in China.

Picture Credits: t=top, b=bottom, c=centre, l=left, r=right, OFC=outside front cover, IFC=inside front cover, IBC=inside back cover, OBC=outside back cover.

The Advertising Archives; 30tr. Archive Durand-Ruel; 25/25cb, 30bl. The Barnes Foundation; 31tr. Bridgeman Art Library; OFC (main pic), 8/9t, 15cr, 19bl, 20bl & 20tr, 23t, 25tl, 26l. Giraudon; 2/3t, 4tl, 4bl 4/5t, 6/7t & OFC, 6/7b, 7l, 8bl, 9cl & 9br, 10cb, 10/11t, 10/11b, 11tr & OBC, 12bl & OBC, 12/13t, 13cl, 13br, 14bl & 14/15t & 14/15cb& 15tr & IFC, 16bl, 16tl & 16/17t & 17cb & 17bl & 17br & 32ct, 18l & 18/19t & 19br, 20/2c 21tl, 21r, 22tl, 23bl, 24bl, 24tr, 26/27c, 27tr, 27bl & 27br, 28tl, 28/29cb, 29tr, 30br. Mairie de Paris © Photothèque des Musées de la Ville de Paris; 2bl. National Gallery of Washington; 4/5b. Réunion des Musée Nationaux © Photo RMN-Gérard Blot; 22/23cb. Union Centrale des Arts Decortifs; 3r.

Every effort has been made to trace the copyright holders and we apologise in advance for any unintentional omissions. We would be pleased to insert the appropriate acknowledgement in any subsequent edition of this publication.